Meeting Management

90 Minute Guides

Michelle N. Halsey

ISBN-10: 1-64004-026-9
ISBN-13: 978-1-64004-026-7

Contents

Chapter 1 – Planning and Preparing

You are on your first project and you have to organize and manage the project kick-off meeting. What do you do first? Do you create the agenda or the invitation list? How do you run a meeting? What preparation do you need? All of these are valid and real questions you, as the meeting manager, must address. There is no doubt about it. Meetings require skill and technique in order for the meeting to achieve its purpose. Disorganized and poorly managed meetings waste time and hurt your credibility as a meeting manager. Consistently leaving a poor impression with the attendees will haunt you if left unchecked.

This training course is designed to give you the basic tools you need to initiate and manage your meetings. You will learn planning and leading techniques that will give you the confidence to run a meeting that will engage your attendees and leave a positive and lasting impression. This is a hands-on workshop and your participation will help make it a valuable experience. Use this time to begin the process of developing your skills along with other participants who share the same desire to improve their meeting management skills.

Before we begin, let's get to know each other better. Since we will be spending most of today working with each other, it is worth the time to share some things about ourselves now, making it easier to engage in the course.

By the end of this tutorial, you will:

- Planning and Preparing

- Identifying the Participants

- How to choose the time and place

- How to create the agenda

- How to set up the meeting space

- How to incorporate your electronic options

- Meeting Roles and Responsibilities

- Use an agenda

- Chairing a Meeting

- How to deal with disruptions

- How to professionally deal with personality conflicts

- How to take minutes

- How to make the most of your meeting using games, activities and prizes

Planning and Preparing

The first step in making your meeting effective begins with your planning and preparation activity. Determining the purpose of your meeting, the people who should attend, and the place of the meeting will form the foundation on which you will build your agenda, decide what materials you need, and identify the roles each attendee hold in the meeting. In addition, planning and preparing for your meeting helps to reduce the stress that may result from managing a meeting, because you will avoid unexpected incidents and issues that could derail your meeting.

This module is part one of your planning session, which focuses on important factors that could affect the success of your meeting. These factors are the people, place, and purpose of the meeting. Let us take a closer look to see how we can organize this to your success.

Identifying the Participants

Determining your meeting participants is an important planning step. You should not approach this casually. Who attends your meeting could help or hinder the meeting dynamics. There is a tendency to invite everyone you know in an effort to cover all angles. This is overkill. Before you think about whom to invite, think about the purpose of the meeting. This will help you determine who should be invited. Be specific when determining the purpose of the meeting. For example, if you are meeting to resolve a problem, invite only those who are capable of providing solutions to the problem. Avoid inviting a high-ranking manager, who could thwart solutions before they are developed.

On the other hand, if your meeting is to come to a decision on a policy or product, do not invite people who do not have the power to enact those changes. Having people who cannot contribute to the meeting will exclude them and affect the meeting environment. Identifying the purpose of your meeting first will help to determine who should attend. Here are some common reasons to call a meeting:

- Problem solving

- Decision making

- Conflict resolution

- Project initiation

- Planning

- Brainstorming

Once you determine your meeting purpose, you can list all the names of the participants you wish to attend. Once this list is created, then determine what each participant will contribute to the meeting. If a participant is deemed a non-contributor, they should be removed from the list. When all non-contributors are removed, you should have a good list of participants for your meeting.

Choosing the Time and Place

There are several considerations you must address when planning the time and place of your meeting. For instance, the time of day is essential if your meeting is meant to be a brainstorming session or problem-solving meeting. Setting these types of meetings right after lunch or late in the day could be a frustrating experience. Humans after lunch are usually lethargic and meetings at the end of the day are plagued with participants looking at the clock in anticipation to leave work and go home.

Meetings that require energy and high level of participation are best scheduled between 8 and 9 AM in the morning. Most workers are not engaged in their daily work yet so you will have their attention and energy for use in your meeting. The next best time for a meeting is around 3 PM. This gives your participants enough time to recuperate from their lunchtime meal. It also gives you at least an hour of cushion before your participants start thinking about going home. Meetings that are low key could be scheduled anytime during the day. Just remember not to schedule them to close to lunch or the end of the workday.

The location is also important to your meeting dynamics. Try to schedule your meeting in a well-lit spacious room. If you can get a room with windows, do so. Dark and cramped rooms will bog down your meeting. Some people get claustrophobic and are distracted by their surroundings. A couple of other things to consider are the need for privacy or if you intend to have an outside visitor attend. If the meeting topic is of a sensitive nature, then getting a room with more privacy will make participants more comfortable to discuss the issue. Furthermore, if you plan to have an outside visitor attend your meeting, get a room that is closes to the main entrance. This way your visitor does not have to search the halls of your organization in search of your meeting.

Creating the Agenda

Creating the agenda can be easy if you know what to do in advance. The **SOAP** technique helps to collect the topics, organize them, and select the ones that will contribute the most to your meeting.

Seek topics from your participants: send an email to the list of participants you created, asking for agenda topics. Give a brief explanation of the purpose of the meeting and an idea of what you are looking for in terms of topics. Do not make this the formal invitation. When you make the request, make sure you ask the participants for the time they need to discuss their topic, and provide a deadline to get their topic to you so it can be included on the agenda.

Organize topics into a list: once you receive the topics, organize them into a list along with the time and the name of the presenter. This will give you the ability to scan through the list, narrowing it down to the topics you will select for the agenda.

Assess which topics are relevant to the meeting purpose: with your list organized, determine which topics are the most relevant to the purpose of the meeting. Scratch out those topics you do not intend to use.

Pick the number of relevant topics that will fit into your meeting time: review the time of the remaining topics. Select the enough topics to fill the time of your meeting minus ten minutes. Give yourself ten minutes for meeting overrun. If you go over, you will end on time. If you do not, then you get to adjourn your meeting early, making everyone happy.

Remember to contact the presenter that had their topic removed from the agenda, explaining the reason why it was not put on the agenda and recommending that topic be saved for another meeting.

Gathering Materials

Each meeting you hold will require both basic and special materials. Your job as the meeting manager is to determine what you need and acquire them in advance, avoiding last minute surprises.

The **SHOWS** acronym stands for stationary, handouts, organizer, writing tools, and special requests. Let us break down each letter so you get a better understanding of what this means.

Stationary: this is all the paper you will need at the meeting. It includes, note pads, sticky notes, index cards, envelops, tape, paper clips, folders, and flip chart. Each meeting is different. You do not have to bring everything on this list. Determine what is going to take place at the meeting and materials needed for each activity or presentation. It is also wise to consult with the people on your agenda to see if they are going to facilitate activities that require stationary.

Handouts: many times you or your presenters will need to distribute handouts. There could be a worksheet or an outline from an electronic presentation. In any case, you should consult with your presenters and acquire any handouts they may use. Determine if the handout they are giving you will be the most up-to-date version. If not, have them send it to you when they finalize it. Remember to set the expectation to have it a day or so in advance, giving you time to print and file it in your handout organizer.

Organizer: when it is time to meet, the last thing you want to do is show up with a stack of handouts. Using an organizer like a portable accordion file or Pendaflex is an easy way to file your handouts and other stationary materials in one container. The filing system will allow you to file the documents in an orderly fashion, making distribution of the materials more professional. You want to avoid shuffling handouts around in front of your participants when it comes time to distribute them.

Writing tools: this includes pens, markers, highlighters, and dry erase markers you may need for your meeting.

Special requests: from time to time, your presenters may make a special request. An example could be a poster. Ask your presenters ahead of time for special requests.

Sending Invitations

Many times invitations are sent without much thought. We figure the sending mechanism, whether it is Outlook or any other type of electronic program, will do the job effectively. It is wise to use an electronic tool for your invitation; however, there is more thought that should go into it. The three "P" approach gives a consistent and clear method of structuring your meeting invitation. Here is the breakdown:

Purpose: the purpose of your meeting must be stated up front. It is not enough to put in the subject line: "Planning Session." The vagueness of your purpose could result in low attendance. Be specific with your purpose. Instead of "Planning Session," you could state, "Planning our budget for the first quarter." In addition, you should attach your agenda, which gives more detail of the discussion topics.

Place and Time: determine ahead of time where and when the meeting will take place. Avoid sending out invitations with a to-be-determine (TBD) message. The more effort you place on getting the details done in advance the more your attendees will take you seriously. In addition, provide clear instructions on the exact location.

Pact: create a sense of binding agreement by setting expectations so you get the most responses as soon as possible with a level of commitment. For example, state, "Please respond to this invitation within 48 hours." Also, set a cancellation policy by stating, "If you need to cancel, please call, or email me as soon as possible." You could also include a statement that states, "Upon acceptance of this invitation, you are expected to attend." Finally, you could also include a statement like this, "This meeting is a planning session, and your participation and idea-sharing will be greatly appreciated."

Structuring your invitation with clear and concise information and expectations sends the message that you are seriously managing this meeting. You do not want to be famous for holding boring and inefficient meetings. This is something that takes a long time to correct.

Making Logistical Arrangements

There are several areas where you should be planning the logistics.

Physical space: consider the space in which you plan to hold your meeting.
* Is it on site or off site?
* Do you need to make reservations?
* Does it need to be set up?
* Do you have to contact you facilities department to remove or add partitions?
* Do you need furniture moved?

Travel: identify who will need to travel to your meeting.
* Do they need travel arrangements?
* Do they need transportation to and from the meeting location?
* Do you have to make security aware of their presence so they are not held up at the door?

Food: determine if you need to organize meals.
* Is your meeting starting early in the morning and you need to serve a light breakfast?
* Is your meeting all day?
* Are you going to cater food?
* Are you planning to have lunch at a local restaurant?
* Do you need to make reservations?

Audio and visual: later there will be a discussion on electronic options; however, if you plan to use electronics like a presentation or video.
* Do you have to get this placed in the meeting room?

- Are you savvy enough in troubleshooting technical problems or do you need a technical assistant?
- Do you need a projector, screen, computer, etc.?
    - Do you need a sound system set up so everyone can hear the presenters?

Signage:
- Do you need to get signs, posters, special handouts made up for your meeting?

Chapter 2- Setting Up the Meeting Space

You are now ready to set up the meeting space. There are many things to consider that will determine what needs to be included in your set up. In the last module, you planned for the things you need. In this module, you are going to put it all together. Although this may seem like a trivial step, you should not take it for granted. The difference from an okay meeting to a remarkable meeting could be the small details. Let us begin with the basics.

The Basic Essentials

Having a predefined list for setting up your meeting is a useful tool and we are going to discuss the setup of your meeting using a handout over the next three lessons. In the first section, you will see a simple list of items comprising of the basic essentials in setting up the meeting space. The list consists of the following items:

- Sufficient number of tables and chairs

- Power strips for laptops and other electronic devices

- Audio and visual set up

- Whiteboard with markers and eraser

- Lectern

- Water

- Verify the room temperature is comfortable

- Microphone for large meetings

- Projector

- Laptop

- Verify room is located in quiet and private area

Make sure you get to the meeting place early enough, giving you time to set up the room without the participants seeing you do it. Getting "caught" setting up the room gives the impression that you are unprepared, which could affect your meeting environment.

The Extra Touches

Extra touches make your meeting more meaningful to your participants. Your handout from the last lesson outlines some items you can incorporate in you meeting set up. Let review some of the extra touches:

* Name tents already printed and set up on the tables

* Table with name tags for each participant already printed

* Projector on with a welcome message illuminating on the screen

* Signage outside the meeting room professionally done

* Keepsake or logo item at each place setting

* Music before meeting starts and during breaks

* Folder with all meeting materials inside (i.e. agenda, handouts, etc.)

* Candy or mints at the tables

* Posters or visual aids posted around the meeting room (professionally done looks better)

* Video playing relevant materials on the screen before meeting starts

* Coat rack during winter months

When it comes to adding the extra touches, be sure to gauge the audience and meeting purpose and plan accordingly. You do not want to create a celebratory experience when the meeting is about cutting costs, etc. Otherwise, going the extra mile helps to make your meeting more effective by creating a personalized environment.

Choosing a Physical Arrangement

The types of activities that are involved in your meeting could help you determine the physical setup. However, before you think further on this topic, let us review some basic setups.

- **Conference style seating:** this is the basic long rectangular or oval shaped table. This type of setup is good for short meetings with less than 30 participants. You would use this for small training sessions and close interactions.

- **U-shape seating:** this is a setup where the tables form a U shape. This is effective where face-to-face interaction is desired. This set up also accommodates larger groups.

- **T-Shape seating:** this design sets up the tables in a T shape. This is also used for face-to-face and large group meetings; however, this shape allows for a leaders to sit at the cross point.

- **Classroom style seating:** this type of seating is best when learning is going to take place and the participants need to take notes. This style can be used for both large and small groups.

Knowing the various styles of seating arrangements helps to determine which to use based on the activity. Below are some suggestions:

- Planning meeting: conference style seating

- Product sales training: classroom style seating

- Strategy sharing meeting: T-shape style seating

- Project update meeting: U-shape style seating

The physical arrangement of the meeting room should always focus on providing a comfortable set up where all participants are able to view the presenter, other participants, screens, and flip chart and whiteboards.

Chapter 3 – Electronic Options

'Advancements in technology have made meetings more effective by providing ways of communicating and storing meeting information. Although many new tools are available to help give your meeting that cutting-edge-feel, there are many things to consider when determining electronic options. It is not always imperative to use new technology at your meetings, but having an understanding in advance helps to expand your choices. In this module, you will learn about the latest meeting tools available to you, things to consider and reaching a decision.

Overview of Choices Available

Electronics in meetings bring a wealth of advantages if used properly. Technology has increased the reach of the meeting room into the virtual world. You are capable of connecting with participants anywhere in the world. Technology also expands your ability to disseminate and record information. This lesson presents an overview of the various tools you can employ in your next meeting.

- **Presentation software:** programs like Microsoft Power Point help to organize your materials into one file. Once the information is in the presentation program, you can make handouts that you can give to your participants as an agenda.

- **Electronic whiteboard:** an electronic whiteboard is an efficient way to write and record ideas all with one source. The electronic device acts like a normal whiteboard, but uses special electronic markers. This electronic device also records the items written on the board for referencing later.

- **Web meeting programs:** programs similar to Microsoft Live Meeting allow you to conduct your meeting via the Internet. Voice, images from your desktop, and a web cam view of the meeting room and the individual.

- **Video conferencing**: this dedicated line uses cameras and television screens to connect two or more remote sites into one meeting.

- **Telephone conferencing:** this is a dedicated telephone line where many participants call in and participate in the meeting.

There a many variations of the electronic tools listed in the lesson that you can use. You can have your company purchase these programs or use a pay-as-you-go product from an online vendor. Choosing the type of electronic tool depends on the audience, distance and technological capabilities of the meeting place.

Things to Consider

The most important thing to consider when dealing with electronic meeting tools is your ability to use and troubleshoot them. Many things could affect the performance of the tools. You must be comfortable enough with the technology to deal with the unexpected. In order to avoid embarrassing issues during the meeting, you should test all systems and make sure your Information Technology (IT) department supports them. In fact, you should always run your technology plans with your IT. They may need to do some backend things to help support your video or web conferencing tool. Before you try using a new tool, get some training and practice. Understanding your electronic tool could take some reading and practice. Test the program with someone you know. Practice using the tool in smaller, more personal meetings before you decides to do it in a larger meeting with outside guests.

Avoid using technology just for the sake of using it. Use it only when it is necessary. Make sure that the participants who will need to use the tools to participate are capable of using it themselves. The last thing you want is someone telling you in the middle of the meeting that they do not know how to launch the program. Here is a quick list of things to consider if you plan to use technology:

- Is the complexity of adding the technology outweighing the potential glitches?

- Are you capable enough to handle any issues that may arise during your meeting?

- Is your audience capable of handing the technology?

- Will you have adequate support from your IT department?

- Are there any costs that you have to consider?

In any case, using technology requires knowledge. If you desire to use technology in your meetings, learn the system and practice, practice, practice. Finally, do not get carried away with technology. It becomes obvious when technology is being used just to dazzle the audience. This is distracting and reduces the effectiveness of your meeting.

Making a Final Decision

This assessment allows you to determine quickly if you need to use technology or not. When making a decision determines the following:

- Am I proficient with the technology?

- Am I able to acquire someone who is proficient and can assist me with the technology?

- Will there be people connecting to my meeting from remote locations?

- Is there a large number of graphics that will be presented?

- Are the participants capable of using the technology?

- Does the meeting room support technology?

- Do you have IT support available?

- Do you have the budget to support the technology?

If you answer "no" to any of these questions, determine the risk of going ahead with the technology. If it is too risky, avoid using the technology, unless you must like in the case of remote conferencing. Just make sure you get the training you need well in advance or get someone to be there as a technical helper if technology is unavoidable.

Chapter 4 – Meeting Roles and Responsibilities

Establishing clear roles and responsibilities in your meeting helps to manage the meeting effectively. When roles are established, the participants have a clear understanding of what is taking place because the person in a specific role has a job to fulfill. Assigning roles also alleviates the task you have to manage. This way you can focus on the role you are to manage within the meeting time. Remember that you do not have to do it all. Get others involved.

In this module, you will learn the role of the Chairperson, Minute Taker, and the Attendees. Finally, you will learn how to vary the roles for large and small meetings. Let us begin first by identifying the role of the Chairperson.

The Chairperson

The meeting chairperson is responsible for directing the proceedings of the meeting. They are time managers, referees, and enforcer of the rules when they are broken. The chairperson does not necessarily have to be you all the time, but when you do defer the chairperson's duty to someone other than you, make sure you are confident the chairperson you choose can handle the role. The chairperson must be able to lead the meeting and be firm throughout the meeting.

Here are additional responsibilities of the chairperson:

- Be aware of the rules of the meeting if present

- Keep to the aim or objective of the meeting

- Remain fair with all participants

- Start the meeting

- Transition from agenda topic to the next

- Introduce the next presenter

- Handle disruptions

Some of the qualities a chairperson should possess are as follows:

- They should have some level of authority

- Demonstrate flexibility

- Remain impartial

- Display maturity

The role of the chairperson is essential if the meeting is to have some form of control. If you are the chairperson, make sure you do not take on additional roles. You want to remain focus on the tasks associated with the role of the chairperson. If you select another person to be the chairperson, it is a good practice to meet with him or her in advance of the meeting to coordinate the agenda and set expectations. You want to avoid miscommunication during the meeting, which could hurt the credibility of both your chairperson and yourself.

The Minute Taker

Taking minutes requires some basic skills. For instance, a good minute taker will possess great listening skills, and attention to detail. Furthermore, they should have excellent writing skills and communication skills. The person you select must be able to maintain focus and not be carried away with the meeting, missing crucial meeting information. It is best to select someone who is not directly involved in the meeting, allowing them not to participate. Here is a list of tasks the minute taker should handle:

Before the meeting
- Determine what tool to use for recording the minutes (ex. Laptop, paper, recording)
- Become familiar with the names of the attendees and who they are
- Obtain the agenda and become familiar with the topics

During the meeting
- Take attendance
- Note the time the meeting begins
- Write the main ideas presented in the meeting and the contributor of that information
- Write down decisions made and who supported and opposed the decision
- Note follow up items

- Note items to be discussed in the next meeting
- Note the end time of the meeting

After the meeting
- Type up the minutes immediately after the meeting (if manual notes or recordings were taken)
- Proofread the minutes and correct any errors in grammar and spelling
- Save or send the document to the meeting owner

Using a template helps to keep the minute taking consistent. Remember to meet with the person you choose to be your minute taker before the meeting to go over the template.

The Attendees

The attendees are not excluded from assuming a role or having a responsibility in the meeting setting. Of course, you cannot force the responsibility on to your attendees, but you can attempt to influence them. The attendees are the biggest success factor of your meeting. If they feel that they accomplished something in the meeting, they will applaud you. However, if they walk away feeling they wasted their time, this could affect your credibility. The following are responsibilities your attendees could assume:

Prepare
- Be prepared to contribute to the meeting
- Be prepared to arrive early and avoid being late
- Be prepared for the meeting by jotting down ideas and questions ahead of meeting
- Be prepared by reading the agenda before the meeting
- Be prepared for a long meeting by getting enough rest the night before

Participate
- Ask questions
- Take notes
- Share ideas

Productive

- Avoid carrying side conversations
- Remove distractions like cell phones and PDA's
- Keep to the allotted time if on the agenda

Setting up expectations is the best way to communicate the role of the attendees. This is accomplished in either the meeting invitation, or separate email to the attendees. In any case, it is worth the time. Remember that all participants play a vital role in the meeting. Your job is to remind them of their role and the responsibility that comes with that role.

Variations for Large and Small Meetings

Large meetings present very different dynamics than smaller meetings. Managing a larger meeting requires more resources and assigned roles. If you are chairing the meeting yourself, you will need to rely on others to ensure all things are well executed. Here is a list of additional roles you may want to add when managing a large meeting:

- An extra minutes taker for better accuracy

- A person to distribute all the materials related to the meeting

- A person to greet attendees

- A person to run the audio and visual equipment

- A person to manage the hospitality aspect of your meeting

- A co-chairperson

- A person managing the presentations

On the other hand, in small meetings, you can assume multiple roles. For example, you can be the chairperson, technical person, and the minute taker in a small meeting. Small meetings are less formal and you can leverage the informal environment to multitask. You may need an assistant if the meeting is comprised of important people. In any situation, careful planning and assessing the risk of working with less roles will help you to determine what roles need to be filled. When in doubt, get more help. Err on the side of caution.

Chapter 5 – Chairing a Meeting

Chairing the meeting is a leadership role. You must be ready and able to stand up and kick off the
meeting without sounding nervous or uncomfortable. Your ability to communicate early in the meeting sets the tone of the meeting. Chairing a meeting effectively takes time to develop and requires practice.

This module is part one of two modules that teaches how to effectively chair a meeting. The first part, will teach how to start your meeting on the right foot. Next, we will discuss the role of the agenda and finally, we will discuss how to use the parking lot. All these techniques are designed to make you a more effective chairperson. In fact, you will get an opportunity to practice commencing a meeting. Do not worry. This is a safe learning environment where you will not be forced to do something you are not comfortable doing. However, remember to use your action plan if you need more practice chairing a meeting. Let us start this module from the top, which is getting off on the right foot.

Getting Off on the Right Foot

Opening your meeting effectively requires both a technique and a flow. The **SIGNALS** flow gives you an easy model to follow when opening the meeting. Here is a breakdown of the acronym:

- **Salutation** is opening the meeting by welcoming and greeting your participants

- **Introduction** is where you introduce who you are

- **Guest mentioned** is where you introduce those attendees that are special guests

- **Need-to-know** is a list of things like logistics, bathroom location, fire exits, general meeting format that is shared with the attendees

- **Agenda** is where you discuss the purpose of the meeting and give a brief overview of the agenda

- **"Laws of the meeting"** is where you discuss how the meeting is going to run. This includes policies on electronic devices, participation, and handling conflict.

- **Segue** is the part of your introduction that links this part to the next topic, which in this case will be the role of the agenda.

Practicing your opening is the best way to become better at it. Over time, you will develop your own style, which will be comfortable to you. In any case, you will need to do it in order for you to learn it.

The Role of the Agenda

The agenda is an entity that plays a vital role like the chairperson or minute taker. Is should not be ignored, because if it is ignored, your meeting will experience time and participant management problems. Many times meetings run over or are cut short leaving topics unaddressed that were on the agenda. Consistently missing the agenda time and topics is a sign of poor meeting management. Here is a list of items the agenda accomplishes when handled as a role at the beginning of the meeting:

The agenda communicates:
- Meeting topics
- Presenters
- Time allotment for each speaker

The agenda provides focus by:
- Stating the meeting objectives clearly
- Outlining the meeting in increments of time
- Providing a checklist of things to accomplish in the meeting
- Allowing the attendees to see both the beginning and the end of the meeting, avoiding them becoming distracted when they are left wondering when this meeting end will

Here is a sample introduction of how to introduce the agenda as a role at the beginning of the meeting:

"The agenda today will help us meet today's goal of deriving a good sales strategy. We have four presenters who are going to discuss how to present the new product, handle objections, gain commitment, and

close the sale. The agenda will be our guide so we can stay on track and finish on time."

Simply handing out the agenda does not communicate its role. You must introduce it like any other person that has a role in the meeting.

Using a Parking Lot

Using a parking lot in your meetings provides a place where topics that cannot be answered during the meeting are noted for follow up later. Sometimes the topics in the parking lot may be answered during the course of the meeting, but this is unusual. The parking lot is simple to implement. You could create a physical place by using piece of flip chart paper with sticky notes. Perhaps you prefer electronic documentation. You can collect parking lot topics onto a spreadsheet. Whatever you choose, you need to have a basic format. Here are some things to consider:

- Take a few moments to share with the attendees how the parking lot works
  - o Meant for topics that require follow up after the meeting
  - o Hold questions that can be answered later in the meeting

- Provide brief instruction on how to register a parking lot issue
  - o Provide the question or topic, name, and contact information, on a sticky note or verbally to the minute taker
  - o Chairperson will review parking lot topics to determine if the topic requires follow up after the meeting.
  - o Follow up communication will be sent to all the members of the meeting

The parking lot is helpful in managing your time. It gives you the ability to move off a topic that requires more research and time to develop. Remember to check the parking lot at the end of the meeting and always be sure to follow up when you say you will.

Keeping the Meeting on Track

In order to keep your meeting on track, you should set clear expectations on how time management will be used in the meeting. Setting expectations up front avoids surprised and indignation from the presenter, because they are not caught off guard. In addition, as a chairperson, you must feel comfortable interrupting the presenter when necessary. Many times the presenter would like to be told their time is up. This way they do not have to worry about time. The **STOP** technique helps to keep your meeting on track by doing the following:

Set expectations: letting your presenters and attendees know you intend on managing the agenda vigorously removes the element of surprise. When you neglect to set time management expectations, you are subject to an array of reactions from the presenter and attendees. It may be taken as rude behavior. It does not have to be that way. Let the presenter know that you will give them a signal at five and two minutes remaining. In addition, set expectations for questions and answers. Telling attendees to write their questions down to be asked at the end of the presentation avoids unnecessary interruptions, potentially side tracking the conversation.

Time the presenter: using a timer is the best way to manage the time of your meeting. Keep to the allotted time for both the presentation and the question and answer activity. Always provide a warning time so the presenter does not have to stop abruptly.

Overcome fear of interrupting: perhaps you do not have a problem with this, but there are many who see interrupting someone as rude and find it difficult to do. The best way to overcome this is by setting those expectations upfront. This way you know the presenter is expecting an interruption. The same holds true for questions being asked. If left unchecked, you could lose a lot of time by allowing excessive questions. Use your parking lot to hold questions that require more thought in answering. Call time on questions and answers so you can move to the next topic.

Politely warn people time is nearing: avoid being harsh and rigid. Treating others with respect is the best way to keep the meeting moving and with plenty of participation. You do not want them to shut down because you are becoming a tyrant.

Dealing with Overtime

Going into overtime presents several problems. Once the meeting extends beyond its original end time, you will begin to lose the attendees' attention. This is particularly obvious in large meetings. No matter what size meeting you are dealing with, the goal to dealing with overtime is to acknowledge it before it happens. Look at the agenda and determine if you will need to go over. If you do, then do the following to mitigate the effects of going into overtime:

- Determine your constraints
    o Is the room or venue available for overtime
    o Do attendees have to travel and cannot stay

- Warn attendees in advance that the meeting will over run

- Determine how much more time will be needed

- Communicate the extra time to the attendees

- In a small meeting, gain consensus to go into overtime

- Give choices
    o In a large meeting, provide a brief break at the normal end time so those who have to leave will do so during the break and not the meeting
    o In a small meeting, allow those who need to leave to do so

- If overtime is not an option, determine what agenda items will be missed and plan an alternative way of getting the information to the attendees
    o Follow up email
    o Topic saved for next meeting

If you do not manage overtime, then you will see frustration build among the attendees. Have a plan in place so you know what to do once you determine if your meeting is going to run longer than expected.

Holding Participants Accountable

In a meeting, it may be difficult to hold participants accountable. Participation, questioning, and preparedness could easily be overlooked. Holding your participants accountable involves communication.

Here are three basic steps you can take to holding your participants accountable:

Step 1: Set your expectations: in advance, perhaps in your invitation you should outline what you expect from the participants in this meeting. You may need them to bring questions, or help by providing information. You may want them to participate with vigor. In any case, you must outline what you expect of them before you can hold them to a standard or expectation.

Step 2: Clarify the consequences: let the participants know how you plan to hold them accountable. Perhaps you can warn that you will be calling on everyone for answers. You may also leverage their manager if applicable. You may say that you will be sending the meeting minutes to their supervisors where they can see if they participated or not.

Step 3: Follow through: if you said you would do something, then you have to do it. Do not get into the habit of making empty threats. People will respect you and will naturally be accountable to you because of your work ethic.

Most participants do not want to be on the "bad" side. They want to contribute. Your ability to assert yourself and communicate with clarity your expectations, consequences and determination will make this an easy process with practice.

Chapter 6 – Dealing with Disruptions

Disruptions in the meeting are bound to happen. Personal technology keeps participants constantly connected to the outside world. Frequent disruptions could impede the effectiveness of your meeting and become distracting to those who are focused on the meeting. Furthermore, poorly managing disruptions will reflect on the chairperson or meeting organizer. The key to mitigating disruptions is to plan for them and setting expectations.

In this module, you will learn how to deal with participants constantly running in and out of your meeting, cell phones, off topic discussions and conflicts. The goal is to reduce the affect. It is very difficult to avoid these distractions. It is human nature. Let us begin the module with a lesson on how to deal with participants constantly leaving the meeting.

Running in and Out

Constant disruptions caused by attendees running in and out of your meeting will affect the experience for the other attendees. We often take it for granted that attendees will stay in the meeting and not leave. Therefore, we do not discuss this issue very often at the beginning of the meetings. Addressing this form of distraction is best done proactively. Using the **SIT** technique helps your set the expectation regarding running in and out of the meeting. Next, incorporating frequent breaks lessens the changes of participants leaving the room, and finally giving timely feedback to those who break the rule is necessary in order to stop frequent violators. Let us review each step in more detail.

Set expectations: tell your participants at the beginning of the meeting what you expect of them when it comes to staying in the meeting room. Tell them the effects of constantly running in and out of the meeting on the presenter and other participants. Let all the participants know that if they need to leave the room to do so only if it is an emergency and if it is a severe problem, that they should leave the meeting. They will be more of a distraction if they stay.

Incorporate frequent breaks: at the beginning of your meeting, tell the participants they will get a five-minute break every hour the meeting lasts. Establishing this up front let the participants know when to expect a break and wait until then to call people back, etc.

Timely feedback given to those who break the rules: when you have a person still running in and out of your meeting, it is best to address that with them as soon as possible. If you have a problem participant, quietly leave the room and wait for them outside. Speak with the participant in a respectful manner and tell them that their behavior is disrupting the meeting. Ask if they are experiencing an emergency and if they need to leave. If they are not in an emergency, tell the participant if they could wait until the scheduled breaks to do what they have to do.

Cell Phone and PDA Ringing

Most people know to silent their cell phones and PDA's when entering a meeting. However, they may forget every so often. Your job as the meeting manager is to remind them. Here are a couple of steps you can take to remind your participants to turn off those phones.

- Place signs in the room instructing participants to silence their cell phone and PDA's. They can be humorous and light-hearted. In any case, you will get your message across.

- Make an announcement at the beginning of the meeting instructing the participants to turn off their cell phone or PDA now. The signs are a back-up in case you forget to do this.

- Since the participants will most likely looking at the agenda, place a reminder there too. This way you have several areas where the participants can get the message.

One cell phone or PDA going off in the middle of the meeting could lead to a disruption that could last a couple of minutes. You can reduce this type of disruption by almost 100 percent by just mentioning it at the beginning of the meeting and providing reminder signs.

Off on a Tangent

This is by far the most difficult to manage in a meeting. The biggest challenge is to redirect without offending the participants. Using the **EAR** technique helps to do this in three simple steps.

- **Engage the conversation by becoming contributor for a moment.** The goal is not to carry the conversation, but to gain some control by getting the meeting floor. Once engaged you are able to go to the next step.

- **Acknowledge that the topic is valid and worthy of discussion.** This should be a short and affirming statement. This avoids embarrassment of those who carried the conversation when it is time to redirect.

- **Redirect the participants back to the conversation.** This brief statement ends the last discussion and starts up the previous one that was on topic.

Here is a sample **EAR** script:

Participant on a tangent: *I think pizza for breakfast is the best! There is now doubt about it.*

Meeting manager: *I am willing to try pizza for breakfast. It can't be that bad.*

Meeting manager: *Perhaps you represent a large number of pizza lovers that enjoy the same thing you do. I won't knock it until I try it.*

Meeting manager: *Now, let's get back to the problem of employee morale in the call center. Who has some ideas they can share?*

Granted the topic was embellished, but this last script demonstrated the steps clearly. Using EAR will help you master the meeting room every time the conversation goes astray.

Personality Conflict

Sometimes a meeting could result in conflict. This may be true of meetings where new teams are storming together and forming the team. Conflict could arise when two participants with opposing views clash. In any case, conflict in a meeting has to be managed. There is an acceptable degree of tension, which is normal in debates. However, when the tension turns in to outright conflict, the focus turns from the meeting to the spectacle that is the conflict. Your job as a meeting manager is to diffuse the conflict and restore order in the meeting. Allowing conflict to go unchecked could fester into a bigger problem for everyone in the meeting. The news of the conflict will spread quickly and how you managed, it will be scrutinized. Here are three steps to take when conflict arises.

Step 1 Stop: Stop the conflict by intervening and making a statement that acknowledges the conflict. Do not become frustrated yourself. Avoid taking sides. Never yell. Be professional and calm. Simply state that the discussion has turned personal and that it needs to stop.

Step 2 Drop: instruct the parties in conflict to drop the discussion for now and regain their composure. There is no need to carry on if the discussion is counterproductive.

Step 3 Roll: roll into a break. Even if you just got back from one, take a break and send the participants away for a moment. Call on the parties in conflict and hold a brief expectations meeting. You are not there to resolve personal conflict. However, you must manage the conflict because it is your meeting. Tell the persons in conflict that they must immediately stop the behavior. Restate the need for the meeting and that healthy debate is always welcomed. Have them agree to behave for the remainder of the meeting.

The meeting room is no place to try to resolve the deeper issues of the conflict. On the other hand, if the participants are all a part of a team that will meet regularly, then this issue has to be addressed in a coaching session and not in front of spectators.

Chapter 7 – Taking Minutes

Earlier in this course, we discussed the important of the minute taker. In this module, you are going to learn the details of how to take meeting minutes. First, we are going to discuss the purpose of the meeting minutes. Second, we are going to discuss what to record throughout the meeting and finally, we are going to review a template that will help facilitate the minute taking process.

What are Minutes?

Minutes record major points, decisions, and follow up actions that are a result of the meeting. Meeting minutes also help to keep the meeting on track, because it uses the agenda as its outline. Meeting minutes serve as historical data that can be referenced in case a dispute should arise. They are also used to set the topics for discussion in the next meetings. Many times people who could not attend a meeting ask for the minutes so they can be updated on the latest developments in the meetings.

The minute taker should not have a major part in the meeting themselves. They must focus their attention on what is being said instead of participating. With this said, the act of taking minutes does not require that every word that is said must be recorded.

When taking notes, avoid becoming bogged down with writing full paragraphs. Outlining your points will make your note taking more efficient. When you are done taking minutes, immediately proofread and send them to the chairperson and distribute to all the meeting participants. File your minutes for referencing later.

What do I Record?

Many times people think taking minutes is a daunting task because there is a belief that every single word must be documented. If this was the case, then all you have to do is use a recorder and you are done. Recording everything will only make the minutes useless. The idea is to record information about who attended this meeting, the results and follow up action items. Here is a list of items that should be recorded in the minutes:

- Date, time and place of meeting

- The goal or purpose of the meeting

- The chairperson's name

- Action items assigned to someone for completion after the meeting

- Decisions made during the meeting

- Attendees present and not present

- Items that did not get resolved

- Items to discuss in the next meeting

- Items that were on the agenda that did not get discussed in the meeting for one reason or the other

- The meeting end time

Keeping to this short list will make taking minutes more efficient and useful.

A Take-Home Template

Using a template for your meeting minutes brings consistency to your technique. When you have a template, you can share it with some else, increasing the likelihood of getting similar results. Templates can be either electronic or printed. Incorporating a template for taking minutes also saves, you time by reducing the amount of time formatting the document for distributing to the meeting attendees.

Chapter 8 – Making the Most of Your Meeting

Many times, meetings can be seen as boring events that people have to attend. That does not have to be the case. You can incorporate various elements into your meeting, which could make your meetings more interesting. Making the most of your meeting does not have to involve a lot of preparation. It just requires creativity and imagination. Let us learn some ways we can make our meetings fun.

The 50 Minute Meeting

The reason why meetings usually last an hour is that our computer program that sets up the meeting usually has 30-minute increments of time. We are forced to schedule meetings to last at least an hour. On a daily basis, we attend more 1-hour meetings than any other kind. When you have several meetings in a row that last an hour each, you will find that you do not have time to check your emails or do other things in between because the next meeting starts right on the hour. The 50-minute meeting is an effective way to space out meetings, allowing us time to do things in between meetings. Conducting 50-minute meetings takes discipline in time management. Here are four steps to make the most of your 50-minute meeting:

Step 1 Have an agenda: We discussed the importance of having an agenda. The agenda is the document that outlines what will be discussed in a specific amount of time. With an agenda, you will have the group agree on what topics for discussion. Send out your agenda ahead of time so your participants get an idea of time spent on each topic.

Step 2 No side conversations: Set the expectations with your participants that side-conversations are not allowed and that you expect them to be fully engaged in the meeting. Blackberries, iPhones, etc. are not allowed and express that you will hold them accountable if you see people looking under the table at such devices.

Step 3 Summarize actions steps: At the end of the meeting, summarize any action steps that resulted from the meeting. You should have action steps at the end of the meeting. If not, rethink why you held the meeting in the first place.

Step 4 Send out summary notes: This is the meeting minutes. This should be done as soon as possible after the meeting. Sending out the meeting notes is a great way to solidify those action items with the people responsible for doing them.

Using Games

Using games in meetings helps to increase productivity. Many games could be used in meetings. We recommend you research the bookstores and find a resource that outlines appropriate games you can use. Remember to think about the meeting purpose before you use a game. If the meeting is about budget cuts, then you do not want to use a game in that type of meeting. Meetings that form new teams or launches a new product is best suited for games. Furthermore, determine how much time the game will take to complete versus the entire time you will be in the meeting. You do not want to play a 15-minute game in a 50-minute meeting.

Here are some Do's and Don'ts when it comes to using games at meetings:

Do's

- Do use games from a book or legitimate resource

- Do use games for meetings that are meant to form new teams

- Do gauge the amount of time the game takes to play against the entire meeting time

- Do practice the game before you use it

Don'ts

- Do not use games in serious meetings

- Do not spend too much time on the game

- Do not make up a game of your own (unless you are confident you can pull it off)

Giving Prizes

Prizes in meetings should be used to reinforce positive behaviors. The prizes do not have to be extravagant. They could be pens, desk decorations, t-shirts, etc. When giving prizes away, be clear on how to win the prizes. Unclear instructions will lead to outbreaks of conflict when someone feels cheated. For example, if you announce that a person will get a prize for coming back from break on time, almost 95 percent of the time you will have some stay in the room and not go to break to win the prize. Make it clear that they have to leave the room. Perhaps you can up the challenge by stating that the person coming back to the meeting who is the closest to the break end-time without going over will win.

Here are some ways you can leverage prizes in your meetings:

• The most participation

• The first to arrive at the meeting

• Volunteering for something in the meeting

• Creative solution

• Who can recap the action items the best

There are no limits on how to use prizes at your meetings.

Stuffed Magic

Simple magic tricks can help reduce stress and create a fun meeting environment. Before you start doing magic tricks in meetings, you will need to practice them at home. Magic tricks work well only when they are done right and with confidence. The setting up of the magic trick is the most important aspect. Do not be eager to do the trick or make an announcement. Be calm and natural. Incorporate it into the meeting seamlessly. You do not want to stop and announce you are going to do a trick. When participants are taken in by the trick without knowing, the effects are greater.

Research books and the Internet for magic tricks you can use. Practice the tricks and use them in the appropriate meeting settings. Try to avoid tricks that could embarrass others. You want to create an environment that is safe and offending someone could hurt that environment.

Additional Titles

The 90 Minute Guide series of books covers a variety of general business skills and are intended to be completed in 90 minutes or less. It is an effective way for building your skill set and can be used to acquire professional development units needed by project managers and other industries to maintain their certification. For the availability of titles please see https://www.silvercitypublications.com/shop/.

No. 1 - Appreciative Inquiry

No. 2 - Assertiveness and Self Control

No. 3 - Attention Management

No. 4 - Body Language Basics

No. 5 - Business Acumen

No. 6 - Business and Etiquette

No. 7 - Change Management

No. 8 - Coaching and Mentoring

No. 9 - Communications Strategies

No. 10 - Conflict Resolution

No. 11 - Creative Problem Solving

No. 12 - Delivering Constructive Criticism

No. 13 - Developing Creativity

No. 14 - Developing Emotional Intelligence

No. 15 - Developing Interpersonal Skills

No. 16 - Developing Social Intelligence

No. 17 - Employee Motivation

No. 18 - Facilitation Skills

No. 19 - Goal Setting and Getting Things Done

No. 20 - Knowledge Management Fundamentals

No. 21 - Leadership and Influence

No. 22 - Lean Process and Six Sigma Basics

No. 23 - Managing Anger

No. 24 - Meeting Management

No. 25 - Negotiation Skills

No. 26 - Networking Inside a Company

No. 27 - Networking Outside a Company

No. 28 - Office Politics for Managers

No. 29 - Organizational Skills

No. 30 - Performance Management

No. 31 - Presentation Skills

No. 32 - Public Speaking

No. 33 - Servant Leadership

No. 34 - Team Building for Management

No. 35 - Team Work and Team Building

No. 36 - Time Management

No. 37 - Top 10 Soft Skills You Need

No. 38 - Virtual Team Building and Management

www.ingramcontent.com/pod-product-compliance
Lightning Source LLC
Chambersburg PA
CBHW071436200326
41520CB00014B/3720